The Spiritual Experiences of Hospice Nurses

LAWRENCE JAMES

NEWMAN SPRINGS PUBLISHING
320 Broad Street
Red Bank, NJ 07701

First originally published by Newman Springs Publishing 2023

ISBN 979-8-88763-435-7 (Paperback)
ISBN 979-8-88763-436-4 (Digital)

Printed in the United States of America

To my deceased mother who was killed by a drunk driver. She never had the opportunity to live a full life and died peacefully, comfortably, and out of pain, with her family and friends at her side.

Also, to my two sisters who protected and cared for me when I was very young. Their names are Kathleen and Maureen.

Contents

Introduction

IN THE UNITED States today, we have developed and continue to improve care for people who are dying. Hospice provides the support that family and friends need. Hospice palliative care is a team effort to affect a peaceful pain-free death for the patient.

You will see in this book the skills hospice staff provide for the patient, family, and friends. The patient is cared for medically, physically, psychosocially, and spiritually. A peaceful death demonstrates how hospice provides the services people need.

After someone passes away, are they just dead, or are they on their way to a spiritual journey to heaven like Christians believe? Also, hospice is constantly learning avenues that other religions believe in where people go when they die. Hospice is constantly learning how to support and care for different cultures from around the world.

My first experience with a dying patient in hospice was in 1988. The company I was working for provided infusion services and had contracted to provide those services to hospice patients. I went to a nursing home where a sweet elderly female was dying of ovarian cancer. I started an IV and hooked her up to a mini-infusion pump on a continuous low-dose drip of morphine. The next morning, I went back to the nursing home to assess her pain level and provide further instructions to the nursing home staff. My patient was sitting up in bed eating her breakfast. Her pain level was a 2 on a 0–10 pain scale: with 10 being the highest level of pain on the scale. I saw a dramatic decrease in the patient's pain. Her family was at the bedside and thanked me for getting their mother out of pain. The patient was laughing and socializing with her family. This sweet lady was still dying. However, her quality of life while dying was dramatically improved. Becoming aware of true pain control and quality of life at the end of life changed my whole approach to end-of-life care.

Encompassed in this book are experiences that have impacted me and other nurses and staff providing care for dying patients. Speaking for myself and other colleagues, these experiences have been the most rewarding in our careers.

The actual stories you will read are about how hospice functions and how it provides the highest quality and continuity of care to our patients' families and friends, stories that have a spiritual component that other nurses have told me about and their patients' experiences at the edge of the end of life.

Three of the nineteen stories in this book are mine. However, I will not tell you which ones are mine. No actual patient names will be written. It will be written as the patient, father, mother, and friends. I will maintain the patient's right to privacy and will never sway from that by revealing their names.

The main goal is to provide quality palliative care through symptom management. We manage the physical symptoms and psychosocial problems and assist with the spiritual component of dying. It is total and complete interaction with the dying patient by the hospice team.

All people deserve to die peacefully free from pain. This also depends on the experience of staff, education, training, and geographical area of the country. Services are provided and may be limited to the skills of the staff. Some areas do lack the tools needed to assist people to a pain-free comfortable death. However, in our great country, we continue to strive forward.

When caring for patients, staff will always assess. Were all applications developed to provide pain-free care and assist family and friends in the dying and grieving process implemented? Were they assisted socially and spiritually when needed? Did pain control keep the patient free of pain? Were all the modalities needed implemented to truly help the patient, family, and friends who are having a hard time during and after the patient has passed away?

There is a problem that happens a lot—denial! In hospice, we have the skills to assist people in a peaceful comfortable death. It is not uncommon for people to purposely avoid the discussion of death. Usually, it is a family member and not the patient who is in denial. Denial interferes with providing the services needed for a peaceful comfortable death. It does happen, and usually, it is a family member who will not accept the end of a loved one's life. The nurse, social worker, and pastor will try to help the family member, and still, acceptance is refused. Family members will say, "Let's just not talk about it." That avoidance is incorporated into their denial. Caring for dying patients is intense and is part of the dying process. No matter how hard hospice staff try to educate some family members, they refuse to accept their family member's death and stay in denial. In hospice, we continue to work with these people to assist them through their loss to acceptance of a loved one's death.

In some cases, hospice is just not provided. The patient wants to fight to the end. It is their right to do so. I have seen some of those people who did not give up and made it back. Thank the Lord miracles do happen. However, family members need to clarify what their wishes are to avoid disputes with other family members when the end comes for their family member. I experienced this with a family member in my own family about my father. Sometimes families learn the hard way. Our physical life will eventually come to an end. One cannot escape it. Today physical, emotional, and spiritual care needs are a standard in most healthcare communities.

I always talk about the differences between hospice and the late Dr. Kevorkian. In hospice, we do not kill people. We manage the symptoms of dying so they can have a peaceful comfortable painless death. Spiritual and emotional support is provided by hospice registered nurses, chaplains, pastors, and social workers; all provide the highest counseling inexperience in death and dying. In closing, the stories in this book address the great spiritual journey ahead of us all. Also, it shows you just how the flow of hospice provides amazing care.

Ribs and Beer

THE PATIENT WAS a sixty-three-year-old male admitted to hospice care with a diagnosis of cancer of the spine, for pain control and comfort measures. He previously underwent surgery, chemotherapy, and radiation therapy. All attempts at remission were unsuccessful.

His physician ordered hospice after the patient refused any more treatments. The patient said, "I have had enough of these treatments. I just want to be kept comfortable and die out of pain."

As a young man, the patient went into the trades. He decided to become an electrician. He married his wife, and they had three children, two boys and a girl. Eventually, he became a contractor with a very successful business. In the early days, he and a good friend on Fridays after work would go eat ribs and drink beer. He said, "We became lifelong friends. Our families went on vacations together through the years. Also, we attended the same church. We raised our children as good Christians. They were all baptized by their own choice and accepted Christ as their Lord and Savior. We had some tough times through the years. However, now it seems everything was worth it. All our children have matured well and have made us very happy grandparents. I just really need something for this terrible pain. The pain feels like I am being stabbed constantly with a knife. I was told hospice could get my pain under control and keep me as comfortable as possible."

The patient's wife said, "He has been miserable and just wants to die at home with family at his side. The pain makes him very restless also. He was a hardworking man. He never missed a Sunday at church and is a very devoted Christian, husband, father, and grandfather." The nurse asked the patient's wife, "Is your church pastor aware of your husband's condition?" The wife said, "He is aware and has been visiting three times a week. He does visit more if his schedule is lighter. He has been a great comfort to me also. All the kids go to different churches now. They are spread out across town." The nurse asked the patient and his wife if they would like to have a hospice pastor visit also. They said, "That would be fine. The hospice pastor can help right along with our church pastor." The nurse said, "Our hospice pastors all have a lot of experience in hospice. I'm sure you will appreciate him very much."

The nurse instructed the patient, his wife, two sons, and daughter on hospice services. He said, "You will continue with most of your medications that you have been on. Also, your physician has ordered liquid morphine for pain. A benzodiazepine called Ativan helps with your restlessness. The combination of the two will make you very comfortable. We will start with low doses and increase them to maximize your comfort. We want you to be out of pain and comfortable but not snowed by the medications. As you are aware with narcotics, they cause constipation. Medications for that have been ordered also. It's important that when I visit, you let me know how it's going with your bowels. If you would like I can also insert a catheter. It will make things easier for you and help prevent skin breakdown. As you progress you will become incontinent. I know you're using a urinal most of the time now. It's your decision. You decide." The patient said, "I would like to have a catheter. I'm getting weaker, and it's getting harder just to use the urinal."

On admission, the patient's pain level was a 10 on a 0–10 pain scale with 10 being the highest. After twenty-four hours, his pain level was reduced to a 3 on the pain scale. The patient said, "My wife and daughter give me the liquid morphine every four hours while I'm awake. I take Ativan every four to six hours at a low dose. So far it is working very well."

This was the second visit by the hospice nurse. The nurse said, "I have this flowsheet that I explained to you yesterday. If you ladies could document each time you give him some medication. And if he is conscious, ask him what the pain level is. This way as a team we will know how much to titrate his medications up or down. Also, to the right of the sheet, you can write down when he has a bowel movement. If Colace is not working in your hospice kit, you have two bottles of magnesium citrate. That stuff works well, and it'll clear out those bowels. Hopefully, we will not have to use magnesium citrate. However, it is a very good tool if we need to use it. Constipation as I'm sure you know is not comfortable at all. I know the nurse aide was here earlier. How did that go?"

The patient said, "I feel a lot better. That girl really knows her stuff. She even shampooed my hair with that thing that you put around the head. I'm clean and April fresh. She cleaned the catheter to. She called it catheter care. The hospice pastor is scheduled for 3 p.m. today, and I look forward to meeting with him. My own pastor will come tomorrow. So I will give him the hospice pastor's card, and they can connect."

The nurse reviewed the death and dying process. He left the hospice blue book. It goes completely through how hospice works. He also left information on the dying process by Kübler-Ross.

At 10 a.m. on the fifth day, the patient's wife called the hospice. She said, "I need the nurse to call me. My husband is acting a little crazy." The nurse was notified and instead of calling decided to just go over to the patient's house to get an objective assessment of the patient's behavior. The patient was crying. The nurse asked the patient, "What's going on?" The patient said, "My best friend keeps showing up in a vision. He has a bucket of ribs and a twelve-pack of longneck buds. He keeps saying, 'Come with me.'" The nurse said to the patient's wife, "Can you call over to his friend's house and see if he'll come over and visit your husband?"

When the wife called his friend's wife answered. She was weeping and said, "At 7 a.m. today, he had a massive heart attack and passed away on the job." The patient's wife said, "I'm sorry for your loss. Please accept my condolences. If there's anything I can do to help, please let me know."

Suddenly the patient said, "He's back, and he's telling me to walk into the light." The nurse explained to the patient, "Your friend passed away at 7 a.m. today. His spirit was coming to you to tell you it was okay to let go. He's probably preparing the way for you. So you don't have to be afraid. You have a friend waiting to greet you. And from what most people have told me in their visions, there are a lot of other people whom you've known and loved waiting to see you."

The patient said, "This is very exciting. I pray all the time, and I ask Jesus to forgive me in the times I have doubts. I have had to do this all my life. Now the time is close, and I'm ready to go. It will be a lot better than laying around here in this bed. I just don't want my family to suffer too much. I want them to be happy." The patient told his wife and children to be happy for him. "I have had a good life and I'm very proud of all of you. You, my family, have made my life precious and worthwhile. May God bless you all."

The patient's church pastor arrived. The hospice nurse briefed him on what happened with the patient and also on his physiological status. The pastor went into the room and told the patient, "It's getting close." The patient and the whole family prayed. The wife put on some soft music by Yanni. The patient went to sleep for two days. At the end of the second day, he passed away.

At the funeral services, the pastor reviewed the patient's life. At the closing, he said, "He was a loving Christian, husband, father, and grandfather. Those who knew him always spoke of him as a good family man. He raised his children in the church. He taught them God's Ten Commandments the covenant to live by. He taught them that if they follow the covenants, it would be the sanctification of God's law. He constantly tried to live a clean righteous life. He was an asset to his community and country. We pray now, thy Holy Father and our Lord and Savior Jesus Christ, he be in your loving arms forever amen."

The hospice nurse reminded the family that once a year, the hospice has a remembrance of all the people who had passed the previous year. They would be invited to attend. However, they would not be obligated to.

The End

Angels of Light

THE PATIENT WAS a fifty-five-year-old female admitted to the hospice inpatient unit. Her diagnosis on admission was metastatic bone cancer. All modalities to relieve bone cancer failed, including bone marrow transplant. She decided on hospice care for pain control, comfort measures, and dignity.

The admitting nurse explained to the patient all the hospice services that would be available to her. "Being in the inpatient unit, you will receive total care. Also, your daughter has requested to be at your bedside twenty-four hours a day. We will set up a cot for her to sleep on. Also, she will be able to order meals off the menu here. She will not have to pay for the meals. Our hospice foundation will pay for the meals. In addition to this, a social worker will meet with you to help you arrange mortuary and funeral services and also to provide counseling to any family members that need it. The social worker can assist with other problems you may have." The patient said, "I will definitely need help with mortuary and funeral arrangements. Especially counseling support for my daughter. Also, I do not go to church all the time and do not have a personal pastor. I look forward to meeting with the hospice pastor."

The nurse instructed the patient on her hospice inpatient orders from her oncologist. The nurse said, "Your doctor has ordered you to receive IV morphine in your IV port. You will be placed on the PCA pump. PCA stands for patient-controlled analgesia. You will receive morphine continually through your port on an hourly basis. There'll be a little cord on the pump with a pushbutton. You will be able to push the button for breakthrough pain. The pump is locked out, so all you can only receive medicine for breakthrough pain from the pump every fifteen minutes. The pump was programmed like this to avoid overdosing on morphine. Also, only the nurse can make changes to the pump per the doctor's orders. When setting up the pump, another nurse will double-check and sign off on the settings.

"We believe in safety first. We will start slow and titrate the morphine to a level that reduces your pain and keeps you the most comfortable. We want to keep you as comfortable as possible. However, we do not want to snow you with the medication. Usually, the morphine starts working right away. We rate the pain on a 0–10 pain scale, with 10 being the highest. What would you say your pain level is right now on the scale?" The patient said, "Right now my pain is a 10, and it is horrific. It is stabbing and squeezing so bad I feel like screaming and just want to die." The nurse said, "The medication is here from the pharmacy, so let's just get you hooked up right now." The patient said, "Thank you so much. I really need something to relieve this damn pain. Also, I'm very familiar with the pain scale and know how to use it accurately." The nurse hooked the patient up to the pump and double-checked the settings with another registered nurse. She started a pain control flowsheet to monitor and document progress.

Three hours later, the patient met with the social worker along with her daughter. They found a mortuary and confirmed funeral arrangements. The hospice pastor will perform the eulogy for the patient. The social worker let the daughter know that she would be there for her through the whole process, especially just to talk and verbalize concerns and also to get answers to questions about the dying process. The social worker made sure she had the blue book that the hospice gives out and instructed her on Kübler-Ross's death and dying process. She also gave her one of Kübler-Ross's books. She said, "You can use this book right now for the grief you're experiencing. Also, you can use it for everyday life. For me, it's just an amazing book."

After four hours, the patient's pain was reduced to a 6 on a 0–10 pain scale. After eight hours the patient's pain was reduced to a 4. After twelve hours her pain was a 2. At that time, the patient said, "I should have come here a couple of weeks ago. I feel like eating something tasty. My daughter is picking up spaghetti and meatballs with garlic bread. We are going to have a mother-daughter dinner. We both love spaghetti, and we love to gossip! My daughter is starting to talk like she understands the Kübler-Ross information on death and dying. The social worker has been teaching her a lot and providing a shoulder for her to vent her grief on."

The patient slept all night and only pressed the PCA pump button for breakthrough pain twice. She did not exhibit any signs of restlessness. The next morning the patient visited with the hospice pastor. The patient told the pastor, "I dreamed I was in my childhood home last night. I was in the backyard playing with my dogs. I heard someone say, 'Sweetheart.' I turned around, and there was my mother. She looked like she was thirty years old. She was so beautiful, and she was glowing. She hugged me and told me, "All our past family who had passed away will be here when you arrive. They are excited to see you. Also, several of your old personal friends are waiting to see you. Sweetheart, you will feel peace and love, and everything will be peaceful. There will be no pain or anything to worry about. Tell my granddaughter we will be watching over her always. Tell her she will have a long fruitful life ahead of her. Tell her she should get baptized and except Christ as her Lord and Savior.'"

The pastor spoke with the patient for an hour, and they prayed. The pastor spoke with the patient's daughter and asked her if she wanted to accept Christ into her heart. The daughter said, "My mother told me what my grandmother told her in her dream. Right now, my emotions are screaming all over the place. According to Kübler-Ross, she is right I'm angry because I'm shortly going to lose my mother. I was in denial for a long time. I think she was holding on because of me. I told her I understand now and it's okay for her to let go. I do not want her to suffer anymore. It will be hard to accept her death. I will need your help in counseling pastor to get through this please." The pastor said, "I will be with you all the way. So will the rest of the hospice team sweet child."

The patient spent the rest of her remaining time with her daughter. Her pain level was reduced to a 2 on the 0–10 pain scale. On her fifth day in the hospice patient unit, she went into a coma that morning. At ten that evening, she passed away.

After the funeral, the patient's daughter called the pastor and said, "My mother and grandmother talked to me in a dream last night. They told me to always be kind loving and humble. I want to be baptized and walk in the light of the Lord. I want to accept Jesus Christ as my Lord and Savior and ask Jesus into my heart. I have a lot to learn and need your help. Also, three bright angels of light, beautiful light, told me to stay connected to God through prayer. I told my closest friends, and they looked at me and acted like I'm crazy." The pastor told the daughter, "Some people will never walk in the light of the Lord. However, as your faith grows and you learn more, you may be able to speak to others in a way they will see the Lord." The pastor arranged for the baptismal of the patient's daughter. After being baptized that night, the daughter prayed to Jesus. She asked him, "Please tell my mother and grandmother I have accepted you into my heart, sweet Lord."

At the one-year remembrance at the hospice, the daughter was present. She told the pastor, "I pray every night now that I'm a Christian. I found a good church and have a new family in the Lord. Someday I pray that I will be an angel of light. All things are possible with the Lord thy God!"

The End

Heavenly Express

THE PATIENT WAS admitted into hospice with a diagnosis of endocarditis. He exhibited symptoms of significant congestive heart failure at rest with the inability to carry out the physical activity without discomfort, also symptoms of heart failure at rest and increased discomfort with minimal exertion.

The hospice nurse explained to the patient how the process worked in hospice. He would receive pain medication to keep him comfortable and medication for restlessness. The pain medication would be liquid morphine. Medication for restlessness would be a benzodiazepine, which is also called Ativan. A nurse aide would provide bathing, assistance in eating, and ambulation, if possible, also light housekeeping and meals when needed. A registered nurse would be there to monitor and instruct on medication administration and direct the rest of the hospice team. The social worker would be there to assist with mortuary and funeral arrangements if they have not been arranged. In addition to this, they would contact the family and provide counseling to any family members as needed. Also, a pastor if requested.

The nurse asked the patient, "Do you have a priest or pastor, or would you like to have a hospice pastor visit with you?" The patient said, "I do not have a personal pastor. I'm a truck driver. I have driven in forty-eight states all my life since getting out of the military. I do believe in God, and I pray to him all the time. I believe he has saved me from a lot of close calls. I drove my truck listening to pop and country-western music and eating greasy food at truck stops. That's probably why my damn heart is giving out. I need to speak with the pastor I would really like that."

The patient met with the pastor. The patient said, "After being discharged from the army, I always tried to treat people with respect, even when they were not so nice to me. I always loved diesel trucks as a child. I didn't want to work on them mechanically. I just wanted to drive them. I went to trucking school on the G.I. Bill after being discharged honorably from the army. After my schooling, I landed a job hauling goods and equipment across America. I would listen to pop music and country-western music. It's a great life seeing the country and listening to music driving a big rig. I never married and spent my whole life on the road. I do have many friends in every state. I wonder if they have any big rigs up there in heaven. Could you imagine driving one in heaven? Wow!"

The social worker arrived, and the nurse introduced him to the patient. He asked the patient, "Do you have any family you want me to contact?" The patient said, "I have a younger sister in Ohio. However, she never really wanted anything to do with me after I left and enlisted in the army to go to Vietnam and fight for the liberty of oppressed people. She told me, 'You are a murdering bastard. You murdered women, children, and babies.'

"I told her I never killed women or children. I only killed the enemy who was trying to kill me. I saved a lot of lives in that war, and I never compromised my honor. I never violated the Geneva Convention. I told her that, and she told me to fuck off. That was the last time I saw my sister. I write her letters and send postcards every now and then. I have three post-office boxes across the country. I never received a response from my sister.

"I still love her very much. However, her own beliefs have ruined any potential for a relationship. It really hurts when someone you love hates you. I learned after traveling all over our country God was telling me, 'It's okay. You will be all right.' I prayed and asked God to extinguish her hate. In a dream, an angel told me, 'Some people like your sister will not receive peace until they are ready. Some people never do. She will never truly be at peace until she let's go of the hate in her heart. Keep praying, and someday she will let it go and receive peace and love. You need to know she will eventually accept Christ as her Lord and Savior and repent. She will receive God's grace of love and peace.'"

The social worker assigned to the patient was able to contact his sister. The sister told the social worker, "Yesterday I was visited in a dream. Maybe it was a vision. I don't know if it was an angel. It was a very great white-bluish beautiful light. I could focus on its love and peace. I went to a Baptist Church and spoke with the pastor of the church. I told him I need to be baptized now. I cannot wait." The pastor said, "What is the cause of this urgent need for you to be baptized?" The sister said, "I believe an angel visited me as a bright-bluish light last night and relieved me of my bitterness and hate. I felt love and peace while speaking with what I believe was an angel. I need a pastor to repent for my sins and receive Jesus into my heart. I repented my sins and accepted Christ into my heart as my Lord and Savior. I thank the pastor and most of all I thank Jesus for his love."

The sister said to the social worker, "I would like to be with my brother and care for him until he passes. I have been very mean to him for a long time. I love him and will take care of him until he passes away if it's okay with him." The social worker said, "I believe your brother will be thrilled to hear this and see you. If it's okay with you. I will tell him you are on your way, and you want to take care of him until he passes." The sister said, "I am on my way." The social worker went and told the patient about his sister. He also told the patient about her vision and being baptized. The patient cried and said, "I finally get to spend a little time with my little sis."

The patient's sister arrived, and they both reminisced about their childhood. They prayed together, and she cared for him lovingly. She prayed with him, bathed him, and cooked for him but most of all provided him the love he longed for from her.

Eight days later, the patient passed away with his sister, hospice nurse, and pastor at his side. At his funeral, the VFW performed a six-gun salute and played taps to honor his death. The VFW had contacted some of the men he served with in Vietnam. Four of the men showed up. He saved their life in combat. They said, "He was the bravest man we ever knew. We were able to come home, live normal lives, and raise our families." They prayed over his grave and thanked him for his bravery. Three days after the funeral services, the patient's sister called and spoke with the patient's nurse. She said, "Last night, I fell asleep, and the light returned. It said, 'Oh, who's watching when you get here, sis? I'll take you for a ride in my big rig, the heavenly express.' It's a bright bluish light traveling through the heavens."

The End

War Peace and Love

THE PATIENT WAS admitted to hospice home care for a diagnosis of end-stage renal disease (ESRD). He had been on dialysis for ten years. Also, he had diabetes mellitus and a history of alcohol abuse. He was refusing anymore dialysis, and his serum creatinine was greater than 8.0 mg/dl = milligrams per deciliter. He had decreased alertness with occasional periods of clarity. However, at the time of admission, he was able to answer direct questions with yes or no. He required total care for all activities of daily living. His wife was very fragile and will not be able to care for him at home. The nurse asked the wife if she would be willing to have him admitted to a hospice inpatient unit. She would be able to stay with him at the unit. She could even spend the nights in a cot next to his bed if she preferred. "Also, you'll be able to spend more quality time with him and won't have to wear yourself out physically."

The wife said, "I think it would be best. He is a lot of work, and I love him very much. However, I am very worn down physically and appreciate the help." The nurse called the physician and received orders to transfer the patient to the unit. She also followed the transport to the unit she introduced the patient to his inpatient nurse and helped him get settled into the unit. The inpatient unit nurse called the physician and confirmed orders for the patient. She received the physician orders and services that would be provided in the unit.

At that time the patient became confused. The nurse asked the patient's wife about him. The wife said, "I believe it was alcohol that caused all the physical problems the last twenty years. When he was twenty years old, he was so handsome. He looked like a Greek statue. He went to fight in World War II, and he was a totally different person when he came home from war. He never spoke about his experiences. When people asked him about his experience, he would say I don't want to talk about it. I prefer to just get on with life. I believe he suffered and still does from PTSD. He has nightmares at night. I would wake up at night, and he would be staring out the window. Sometimes he would say I swear I hear Japs out there. Even though he drank heavily, he never missed church on Sundays. Since we married, we never left each other side even through thick and thin."

The nurse told the patient's wife that a social worker and a pastor would be available to her. Her husband and any other family members along with all the staff would help her through the grieving process. Also, the nurse called the patient's family pastor. After speaking with him, he said, "I will be by this evening."

In addition to this, the hospice pastor will be scheduling visits and also be on call when the patient will start to exhibit signs of dying. The social worker met with the patient's wife and helped her arrange funeral services. Also, they found a mortuary. The social worker also contacted the VFW, which will honor the patient at the gravesite. They will provide a six-gun salute and a bugler who will play taps. The social worker asked the patient's wife if there were any family members she wanted her to contact. She said, "I have been calling everyone, and they are waiting for his passing."

On the second day in the unit, the patient's wife decided to go home and get cleaned up. Twenty minutes after she left, the patient walked out of the room and said, "I am looking for Tojo. Have you seen the bastard?" The nurse aide told him, "Tojo's plane had been shot down by a United States Naval aviator, and it was confirmed he was killed in that attack. So you see, sir, nothing to worry about." The patient said, "Thank God we got that murdering bastard." The nurse aide assisted the patient back to bed, and he reported the event to the charge nurse.

The nurse called the patient's wife and let her know they were going to give him a low dose of Ativan, explaining the Tojo incident. Also, the physician had left a standing order to provide a sitter to stay with the patient while his wife was not on the unit greater than four hours. Ativan will help decrease the patient's restlessness and allow him to sleep. The nurse again and impressed to the patient's wife that Ativan will be given at a low dose. It will only be increased if her husband continues to show increased restlessness.

Ativan had to be increased one time and became effective to decrease the patient's restlessness. The patient continued to have short periods of being alert on an off day and night. During the last period of alertness, the patient told his wife, "Thank you for all your love all these years. I had a dream, and an angel from heaven came and spoke to me last night. The angel did a life review with me. The angel told me, 'Even though you did drink excessively, you never tried to hurt people. However, you hurt your wife the most. But she stayed with you due to love. Also, you will receive the Lord's grace.' The grace I will receive is his peace and love. I got to see what I believed was heaven. This sky was the most beautiful blue you'd ever seen. Everything was so strikingly beautiful."

The patient went to sleep after saying this and passed away the next morning. His family and pastor were at his side. At the patient's funeral over two hundred people attended. The patient's wife said, "My husband had so many friends." He would always say, "I believe in God, family, and country These three things are engulfed in love and loyalty. I especially appreciate these two great values. I believe they are the greatest values the Lord has ever given me." The VFW did their salute and the bugler blew taps. The patient's wife said, "I will see you again, my dear sweet love in heaven. Until I make it there, I will see you in my dreams, my only true love."

The End

Comforting Spirit

THE PATIENT WAS a ninety-year-old female. On admission, the diagnosis was metastatic cancer with findings of widespread metastatic disease. On admission, she was alert and oriented. She was able to answer open-ended and direct questions yes or no.

The nurse explained to the patient how hospice works. "The hospice will provide pain control and something for restlessness. The pastor to visit if you approve. Social worker to assist you with mortuary and funeral arrangements if needed. Also, any problems you wish to ventilate or anything you wish to talk about, the social worker can help you. The social worker can assist with other services outside of hospice if you need them. I do not know your situation yet. However, she can get Meals on Wheels set up for you also. A nurse aide will be provided as needed for bathing and light housekeeping."

The patient said, "I will let you know up front I like smoking marijuana and listening to music. I have burial and funeral services arranged already. My best friend is my power of attorney for health care decisions and finances. We have been close friends for forty years, and I trust her more than any other person on this planet. I have lived a long life. When it's time to go, I just want to be kept comfortable and out of pain. You should know I smoke a lot of grass. It keeps me level and helps with pain. My friend will be with me twenty-four hours a day until I die. I have a lot of friends, and they will be coming to visit and say their goodbyes also. However, on the days that the nurse aide comes to bath me, I request that she not leave until my friend gets back from shopping. Also, if she starts to get burned out, I will need assistance to hire a nurse aide so she could have a respite. I would like to have a pastor visit, but a female pastor would be preferred."

The nurse said, "There is a medication not in our formulary called Marinol. I will speak with the physician to see if he will order it. It's synthetic marijuana. Past patients I have taken care of that were on it said it was effective. Since it's not on the formulary, I will ask for what we call an override. This way, no payment for the medication would be necessary. As things progress, if you're on Marinol and you're not getting the pain control you desire, we can switch you to liquid morphine.

"Also for restlessness, there is a medication called Ativan. It's in the class of benzodiazepines. As with Marinol, morphine liquid, and Ativan, we always start you out on a low dose. Then we will titrate up to the safe comfort level for you. We want to keep you comfortable and at the same time not put you in a coma with the medications.

"At one point you will go to sleep and eventually not wake up naturally. It should not be due to excessive medication. Medications for constipation and all your bodily functions will be prescribed and assessable to you and your friend for your comfort. I will review all the medications with you. We use a 0–10 pain scale with 10 being the highest level of pain. On the scale, what would you say your pain level is right now?"

The patient said, "My pain is an 8."

"Tell me after you smoke a joint, what does your pain level go down to?"

"It goes down to a 4, and it lasts for about two hours."

"So you are smoking a joint about every two hours while you are awake. I believe that Marinol will be more effective to reduce your pain than smoking marijuana. I will see right away if we can get that ordered for you. If not, you will be put on liquid morphine, and I will review the instructions on that. I would like to get your pain down to a 1 through 2 on the scale. We will do our best. I promise you."

The patient's physician ordered Marinol for her. Also, an override was given for payment of the medication. He also ordered liquid morphine if Marinol was not effective. At any time she was taking it and it became ineffective, she was instructed to go ahead and start the morphine liquid per protocol.

The nurse reviewed everything with the patient and her friend's power of attorney. They verbalized understanding of the physician's orders and the hospice services. The next day the nurse visited the patient for a follow-up to make sure everything was going smoothly. The patient said, "Marinol is really far out, man. Whoever developed this drug had it together. I am calling all my friends and telling them about it." The nurse asked the patient, "On the pain scale, what would you say your pain level is right now." The patient said, "Right now, it is running between 2 and 4 on the pain scale." The nurse told the patient and her power of attorney, "You should be careful smoking joints now that you're on Marinol. You do not want to overdose." The patient's friend/power of attorney said, "I will make sure she does not do that."

The social worker, pastor, and nurse aide visited the patient. The patient told the pastor, "I had a vision last night. An angel, a very strikingly good-looking man, told me it would be a little over a month until I pass away. He spoke with me about my lifetime. He said, 'You have been a kind and loving person all your life. You figured out at a very young age to stay away from the hard drugs as a lot of your friends did not. We know that you love art. You will be able to create beautiful masterpieces in heaven. I am your ambassador. When you arrive, I will take you around and show you the ropes. You have family and friends who have passed away who will be waiting to greet you. You accepted Christ into your heart when you were thirteen years old. You never backed away from that even after having periods of doubt as you got older. Your future looks bright. In heaven, everything is beautiful and bright.'

"I asked him, 'Why do I have to wait? Why can't I go now?' He said, 'Things happen in God's time, not yours. Do you remember the times you prayed for something from God, and you didn't get it? Those were the times God said no. It's very easy to understand, and you will when you get there.'"

The nurse reminded the POA that once a year, the hospice has a remembrance of all patients they had the previous year that had passed. She would be notified by mail and any other friends who wish to attend. The POA said, "I will create a list to give to the social worker, so you have it on file."

On the RN visit at fifteen days, the patient said, "I keep leaving my body having these out-of-body experiences. That handsome angel is taking me to different areas in heaven. I will enjoy painting a lot of these areas. I'm very excited to go and get started. He told me I will have no more pain. I'll be able to sing and dance anything. Physically I cannot do now. It will be awesome."

On the thirty-fourth day, the patient passed away very peacefully. She did not show a rapid decline; she just passed away. When the nurse arrived, several of her friends and the POA were around her bed. They were all holding hands and singing, "Sweet chariot coming to carry me home."

All her friends who were there said, "When she passed it felt like a peaceful feeling passed through us. Two of us felt an electrical charge." The nurse said, "That was her spirit passing through you." All her friends there said, "Ever since we've known her, she was truly a comforting spirit."

The nurse said, "May she rest in peace. From what I understand, she was a gift to everyone who knew her. I agree she was a comforting spirit!"

The End

Christian Mother, Teacher

THE PATIENT WAS admitted to hospice care for a diagnosis of metastatic lung cancer. It had metastasized to the lymph nodes. She had undergone radiation therapy and chemotherapy and surgery unsuccessfully. She said, "My pain is treacherous. A friend of mine told me that hospice is the best at pain control. I know I am at the end of things. I just want to be out of pain and comfortable while I die."

The nurse asked her, "Do you have anyone else to help care for you while you're at home?" The patient said, "Not really. I have friends who stop by every now and then, but they are really not in any condition to help me. My son lives out of state. His boss told him he can't let him leave work until I die. He said, 'I have too much work to give you a leave of absence right now.'"

The nurse asked her if she would be open to going into a hospice inpatient unit. The nurse said, "I am worried you will fall, or something will happen with nobody around to help you. Also, you will be on pain medications, and you really should not be alone. You would be well cared for, and your pain will be managed by professionals in the unit. We would keep you as comfortable as possible. What do you think about going into the inpatient unit? Also, a staff member can call your son and give him a report on your status every evening. In addition to this, you could talk to your son on the phone." The patient said, "I would feel much safer at the unit. And then my friends could just come and visit me there."

The nurse then called the physician and received orders to admit her to the hospice inpatient unit and arrange transportation to the unit for the patient. The physician said, "I will fax her inpatient orders to the unit now. They will be waiting for her when she gets there." The nurse then arranged transportation for the patient to be transported to the unit.

The nurse then called the patient's son. She informed him of the physician's orders, the phone number, and the address of the hospice inpatient unit. He was also briefed on how hospice works and what to expect. "The staff will call you every evening with updates on your mother's status. This way, you can keep your employer informed in case you have to leave work right away. Hopefully, this will help you on your end." The son said, "Thank you very much. I feel much better now that my mother will not be alone and will be well cared for."

Once the patient was admitted to the inpatient unit, a social worker met with her. They arranged mortuary and funeral services and also compiled a list of friends she would want to attend. The list will be given to the mortuary once you pass so all your friends will be contacted with the date of your service. The social worker asked the patient, "Do you have a pastor or priest who needs to be contacted?" She said, "I have a priest. I would like him to give me the last rites since I'm Catholic. I would not mind meeting with the hospice pastor also. Sometimes you cannot reach my priest at night. You get his answering service. But I know he will make it here to give me last rites before I pass away."

The nurse reviewed her physicians' orders for her. "You will receive IV morphine through your porta cath. Also, a medication called Ativan for anxiety and restlessness." The patient said, "I'm glad I'm here. This is a lot better than I thought it would be. I didn't realize I would have a private room. This is just great here, and everybody is so nice." The nurse told her, "When your son comes to visit, we will set up a cot in the room for him. He can order his meals along with yours if he prefers. Also, you will be on a regular diet and able to eat anything if you can tolerate it. So he could always go out and bring food into the unit for you at times when you prefer."

The patient said, "My son is a master diesel mechanic. I always wanted him to go into medicine or something like that. But he convinced me at a young age he was a gearhead. He loves mechanical things. He understands the physics of machinery. I am very proud of him. He has a beautiful wife and daughter. They attend church every Sunday and praise the Lord. However, he is a Baptist now not a Catholic. His wife made it clear if she was to marry him, he would have to change churches. She feels that the pope is not a substitute for Christ, and she believes you can pray directly to God through Christ and you don't need a priest or an intercessor because we have Jesus.

"I did not object because my son was smitten with her the first day he met her. He is very happy, and there is nothing wrong with that I believe in God's eyes. I know the Lord wants all of us to be loving and kind. Before this cancer started, I retired, volunteered, and tutored young adults to help them get their GEDs. After teaching all my life, it's just in your blood. I am a very straightforward person. I might be a little pushy at times, just so you know. I believe in a way I am very much a naturalist with common sense. Today there are a lot of people who don't know what it's like to work hard and be an asset to their communities."

The nurse reviewed the 0–10 pain scale with 10 being the highest level of pain. The patient verbalized understanding of the scale. She said, "Since this morphine started running, my pain went from a 9 to 3 on the scale. It really makes a difference in pain control. I almost feel like dancing." The patient's son called and said, "I will call every night at eight to speak to the nurse to get a report on my mother. And I will speak with my mother if she is not sleeping. I do not want to wake her up if she is. To wake her up would be mean if she is sleeping, and she is comfortable."

Seven days passed, and the patient was becoming less alert and going into a coma. The patient's son was called at work, and the nurse explained it would not be much longer and that she would pass. The son said, "Would you please give this report to my boss? If he hears it from you, he probably will let me come and be with my mother." The nurse reported to the patient's boss, and he gave him permission to come and be with his mother. Also, his boss paid for first-class tickets round trip for the son. He said, "I am pretty much a hard ass at times. You know I don't mean to be mean to you. But in this business, it is tough, and you have never missed a day's work. A lot of the other guys miss work consistently. You know I appreciate you. So go be with your mother and come back here when you close things out and bury her."

The son arrived at the hospice inpatient unit. The staff reviewed inpatient policies with him. They set a cot up in the room for him. At times his mother was alert, and they both talk about old times. She was more interested in how her granddaughter was doing. The son said, "She loves to go to Sunday school, Mom. She asked to be baptized in the name of Christ. And she's very intelligent, kind, and loving like you, Mom. You gave me such a great childhood even after Dad left. For example, you taught me how to live a good clean life and be an asset to my community. People still have a hard time believing my knowledge base at a young age. I tell them, 'My mother was a teacher. She taught me the value of hard work and common sense.' I love you, Mother, and I will miss our long conversations on the phone. But when you're gone, I will pray to you every night in my prayers."

The following day, the family priest came and performed the last rites. That evening, the patient passed away. Her son, hospice pastor, and nurse were with her. The mortuary was called, and they came and took her away. The son wept and after things settled down; he thanked all the staff and tried to give the charge nurse $2,000 to divide between the staff on the unit. The charge nurse told him, "We cannot accept cash tokens. It is against the hospice policy. However, I can take the cash and donate it in your mother's name to the hospice foundation. I can request that it go for education since your mother was a teacher." The son said, "That makes common sense. Mom would love that."

At the patient's funeral, over three hundred people came to say goodbye. Most of them were former students. They found out through an ad placed in the paper by the social worker. They came to say goodbye to a dear old friend who showed them love and taught them common sense.

The End

Love

THE PATIENT WAS a retired registered nurse and had to go on Social Security Disability secondary to bone cancer. Clinical findings demonstrated malignancy with widespread aggressive metastatic disease, a decline in performance, and significant unintentional weight loss. She preferred palliative therapy.

The patient had received chemotherapy and radiation therapy and refused bone marrow transplants. She requested hospice palliative care at home. She has a nineteen-year-old son in his first year of college. She was a devout Catholic and had attended mass regularly all her life.

The nurse reviewed all the hospice services that would be available to her. She was instructed on symptom management for pain restlessness and anxiety. Also, she was very familiar with bowel and bladder routines since she was a registered nurse.

Her oncologist ordered liquid morphine for pain on a scale that could be titrated up to maximize comfort for the patient. A benzodiazepine Ativan had been ordered to decrease restlessness and anxiety. The hospice nurse reviewed the 0–10 pain scale with the patient. She verbalized understanding of the pain scale. She said, "I have used this scale many years with my patients." In addition to this, "You will have a nurse aide, a social worker, and a hospice pastor if you request one. The whole team will work with you and your son and assist you through the grieving process."

The patient said, "I have several nursing colleagues, my friends who will be rotating shifts taking care of me at home. They are all highly skilled nurses. There will only be a few gaps at times, in which I will need covered assistance from hospice." The nurse reviewed all services with her son also.

The nurse contacted the social worker and set up an appointment for her to meet with the patient. The social worker will meet with the patient at 3 p.m. today. The nurse aide will visit three times a week in the beginning. As the patient will progress, the schedule may be increased if needed. It may not be needed secondary to the fact the patient had friends caring for her who are nurses.

The patient's priest was contacted per permission. He gave his cell phone number to be contacted day or night. He said, "I will be there to give her last rites." The patient also requested for the hospice pastor to make visits. The hospice pastor was contacted and would visit that day. The patient said, "Christ said, 'Whenever two or more people get together in my name, I will be there.'"

The social worker called and confirmed with the hospice foundation that they would provide a nurse aide to be with the patient for the times there were gaps in her care. The hospice foundation authorized payment for those services.

On admission, the patient's pain level was 9 on a 0–10 pain scale. On the second day, her pain level was a 4 on the scale. On the third day, her pain level decreased to a 2 on the scale. Also, on the third day, a low dose of Ativan was started secondary to the patient exhibiting signs of anxiety and restlessness. After starting Ativan along with the liquid morphine, the patient became extremely comfortable and remained alert and oriented and started sleeping more comfortably.

On the fourth day, she started sleeping just three hours at a time. It remained like this until the eleventh day. The patient said, "A voice told me in my sleep that I will soon pass away from this mortal life. He told me the next four days he would be speaking to me about my life. I asked the voice, 'Will this be a life review? I have heard that angels do when you are close and come to do this.' The voice said, 'Yes, it is, and do not worry. The review for you will be a positive thing. In four days, you will enter heaven. You will receive all the gifts that Jesus has promised. You will receive most of all love. All your life as a nurse, you gave your love to thousands of people.' I asked, 'How long will the transition take? I'm ready now.' The words said, 'Once it starts, there is no recognition of time. It is just that you will have to be patient. It happens in God's time, not yours.' I told the voice, 'I'm worried about my son. He is a fine young man and a good devout Christian. I pray he stays on a path of righteousness through Jesus Christ. I asked this for him because I love him dearly.' The voice said, 'You will be able to watch over him until it is his time to come to the Lord.'"

On the third day after the voice had spoken, the patient requested the last rites. They were given by her priest. She told her priest everything the voice had told her. "I will tell you I know tomorrow is my last day. After a visit with my son and my very close friends, it will be the last time. It's rare in this life you have people in your life who never let you down. They all have been that way for me. I love them all so."

The next morning, the patient passed away. She had left a sealed envelope for her son to open on her death. When he opened the envelope written on light blue paper with clouds, it said, "I love you forever, my precious son." Her son wept and said, "I love you, Mother. Thank you so much for everything. Rest in peace."

The End

From Darkness to the Light

THE PATIENT WAS a fifty-nine-year-old male admitted to hospice with widespread metastatic cancer. Eight years ago, he had tumors removed from his neck and right upper chest. He had surgery, chemotherapy, and radiation therapy that successfully put him into remission. Now that the cancer was back and had metastasized to his lymph nodes, he requested hospice.

The patient achieved his MBA by twenty-one years old. He sold stocks and bonds for a brokerage all his life. He had lost his wife to a motor vehicle accident four years ago. He has two children, both girls. Also, his daughters had provided him with the blessing of four grandchildren. On admission with his family at his side, he verbalized, "I want to be kept comfortable and out of pain at home with my family at my side. I would also like a pastor to visit also."

The nurse told the patient, "I will arrange for the pastor to come and visit with you. Also, assign a social worker to assist you with any mortuary and funeral arrangements you need. The social worker will also help counsel family members and help them through everything. A nurse aide will be assigned to assist you with bathing and light housekeeping." The nurse then called the social worker and set up an appointment with the patient and also scheduled the nurse aide with days and times approved by the patient. The pastor was scheduled, and his first visit will be in three hours with the patient.

The patient said, "I had some pretty rough dreams last night. I need to discuss them with the pastor. I am glad he will be here today. It will help me sleep better tonight."

In addition to this, the nurse chose a social worker who had years of experience working with children who had family members who had passed away. She told the patient's daughters, "It would be good to utilize the social worker's skills. You will learn how to present this situation with Grandpa successfully and not harm the children psychologically."

The nurse instructed the patient on hospice care policies and procedures. She instructed the patient on the 0–10 pain scale with 10 being the highest level of pain. The patient said, "I am very familiar with the pain scale and know how to use it." The nurse said, "You will be on liquid morphine for pain and a benzodiazepine called Ativan for anxiety and restlessness. Both are liquids and easy to take. We will start you on a low dose and titrate up to your comfort level without snowing you on the medications. Also, we will establish a bowel routine to try and prevent you from becoming constipated. As you progress, I recommend that we place a catheter. It will help prevent urinary incontinence and skin breakdown. Also, I am leaving this blue book that explains hospice in simple terms. I love this book. It is great. I will come tomorrow at 8 a.m. I want to see how you will be in the morning after receiving your medications overnight. You're very lucky to have your two daughters here to care for you. There is a good book that I read. It says to honor your father and mother."

The pastor arrived at 3 p.m. The patient told him, "Last night, it was so real I fell into a dark pit and could not reach out and touch anything. It was the darkest scariest place I've ever seen." The pastor said, "I have had many patients in hospice who have experienced that. We can pray to Christ and ask him to deliver us from the pit." He prayed, "Our loving Father, we pray to you in Jesus's name to let this patient be free of the pit and be in your loving arms and into your light with eternal peace."

The next morning, the nurse visited to assess the patient's pain level. "Yesterday, you told me your pain was 8 on the scale. What is your pain level today on the scale?" The patient said, "This morning, it is a 4."

At seventy-two hours he verbalized his pain was a 2. On his fifth day, the patient said, "I am out of the pit, and I see beautiful bright lights and a tunnel. It was like I wasn't in my body, and I was floating. When I reached the end of the tunnel, I went into a beautiful valley with people walking around and talking to each other. The colors were so vivid. I've never seen colors as beautiful and peaceful. I am not afraid anymore. I am ready to go into the light and into the valley forever. This feeling was love and peace."

On the sixth day, the patient told his daughters and grandchildren not to worry about him or miss him. He said, "I will be in a very beautiful place, and I will be watching over you and sending you love from my heart."

On the seventh day, Mr. X said, "An angel visited me in a vision last night. He showed me all the good things and bad things I had done in my life. I prayed to God and asked for forgiveness for my sins and accepted Christ as my Lord and Savior."

Two days later, the patient passed away peacefully with his family at his side. The daughters recalled how he was always there for them. He had never really gotten over their mother's death. He often spoke about her and how they met in college. They asked the pastor, "If he would see their mother again." The pastor replied, "He went on his journey to eternal life with the Lord. Also, do not forget there is counseling available to you and your children. Also, remember we have a yearly remembrance at the hospice if you choose to attend. We will send you an invitation just in case. You can call and speak with me anytime. May God bless you and keep you in his loving arms always."

The End

With God All Things Are Possible

THE PATIENT WAS admitted to hospice care with a diagnosis of Alzheimer's. She exhibited an inability to ambulate without assistance. Urinary and fecal incontinence. Her ability to speak was limited to a few intelligible words. Within the last twelve months, she had been diagnosed with aspiration pneumonia and septicemia. Also, she had the inability to maintain sufficient food and caloric intake. In the last six months, she has had a 14 percent weight loss. She had significant dysphagia with recurrent aspirations. She had a history of choking and pocketing food with feeding.

The patient lived with her son and sister. Her son was a mechanic and owned his own shop. He had a good staff working for him and was able to spend a lot of time at home with his mother along with his aunt. He also had retained a nurse aide through a nursing agency. The agency was licensed for home care. The son said, "My mother had me out of wedlock and worked two jobs to support me growing up. I never went without anything. Before Alzheimer's, she and my aunt went to church every Sunday. Growing up it was Sunday school for me. She also had me memorize the Ten Commandments. She taught me to live by them and I do to this day."

The hospice nurse instructed the *son* on hospice services. She also wrote a care plan and reviewed it with the patient's son, aunt, and private caregiver.

The patient had severe agitation consistently at night. Her agitation continued during the day but decreased significantly. The hospice nurse reviewed the patient's medication ordered by her primary physician. Medication was ordered to decrease her agitation and make her more comfortable. The medication was a benzodiazepine called Ativan. The nurse explained, "Ativan is in liquid form, and you can just squeeze the gripper into her mouth. We will start at a low dose and increase it to her comfort level. We want to do this slowly so we don't snow her with the drug.

"In a few days, we should see a significant decrease in her agitation and restlessness. Also, the physician has ordered liquid morphine. You do not have to give this all the time. You know her better than anybody. If she's grimacing or guarding an arm or leg or a spot on her body, she could be having pain. So you could give her a low dose of liquid morphine. It is administered just like Ativan. Directions and instructions for dosage and time limits are on the bottles. If nothing is working within the next two days, I will call the doctor and get further orders. Also, diapers and peri-care supplies will be delivered today. When I visit, I will consistently check your stock of products to make sure you do not run out.

"A nurse aide will be provided scheduled two bathe your mother. She will call and set up a schedule with you. I recommend that you schedule her to your times of greatest need during the day. She can also do some light housekeeping. In addition to this, a social worker will be available to assist with mortuary and funeral arrangements if needed. Also, he is very good to talk to. He has a lot of counseling experience and knows his stuff. Would you like to have a pastor visit also?"

The son said, "I would appreciate that and so would my aunt." The aunt said, "With the pastor here, we can both pray for my sister. What type of pastor is he?" The nurse said, "He is a non-denominational pastor. He will pray with all faiths." The aunt said, "I am looking forward to meeting him."

It took two days to decrease the patient's agitation and restlessness. Ativan worked well and was titrated slowly. Also, every four hours, the son gave his mother a low dose of liquid morphine. The guarding she had exhibited on admission had stopped.

The son said I had a dream last night of my mother. She was younger and told me, "Always live by God's commandments. Also, take good care of your aunt and let love guide you in life's decisions. After I pass away, it won't be long till your aunt passes also. We will both be in the Lord's loving arms. I had to come to you like this due to my physical and mental condition mortally." The son said, "How is this possible, Mother? How is this possible?"

The patient said in her son's dream, "With God all things are possible."

After three weeks, the patient passed away comfortably at home. Her son and sister were at her side. Also, the day before she passed, she told her nephew in a dream, "Please remind my son and tell him all things are possible with God."

The hospice nurse reviewed hospice services with the son and his aunt, such as yearly remembrance of all the hospice patients who passed the previous year. The hospice would mail him an invitation when it gets close to that date. The pastor showed up and prayed with the son and the aunt. In closing, they prayed the Lord's prayer.

The End

Doubts, Fear, Acceptance

THE PATIENT WAS admitted to hospital palliative care for congestive heart failure at rest and refractory angina. He continually had poor responses with optimal treatment of diuretics and vasodilators. Also, he had the inability to carry out physical activities without discomfort, increased discomfort with minimal exertion, and symptoms of angina at rest.

The patient grew up on a dairy farm. After high school, he enlisted in the navy. After boot camp, he trained as a navy corpsman. He served in Vietnam as a corpsman on a naval cruiser. Another word for a cruiser is a destroyer. After being discharged honorably from the navy, he went to college on the G.I. Bill and became a registered nurse. He went to work in an emergency room of a county hospital. He provided emergency care to thousands of people in his nursing career.

The patient said, "My father disowned me because I refused to go back home and take over the family dairy farm." When his mother and father passed away, he and his sister agreed to sell the farm. He said, "I worked hard on the farm growing up and did enjoy the work. However, after serving my country as a navy corpsman, I knew my calling was nursing. It is very rewarding caring for people and nursing them back to health. I especially enjoyed working in the emergency room. It was very fast-paced and challenging."

The patient continued, "I was married and divorced two times. I loved both very much. They both left me for richer and better-looking men. It hurt very much, but I always got over it. I received plenty of fulfillment in my work as a nurse. I did not have any children but have plenty of good friends and a niece and nephew from my sister."

The nurse reviewed hospice services with the patient. He verbalized he was very familiar with hospice services. The nurse made a referral for a social worker, pastor, and nurse aide to schedule visits. The patient also requested that the hospice medical director assume responsibility for his care.

The nurse reviewed all the medications ordered by the hospice medical director. The patient confirmed that they were appropriate. In addition to this, he ordered when your condition worsens you will be admitted into our hospice inpatient unit.

The patient said, "I did not go to church after leaving home for the navy. However, at sixteen I was baptized, and I accepted Christ as my Lord and Savior. I have always believed in God even as a child. I am not afraid of death, and when I pray, I ask forgiveness for the times that I have had doubts. It has been through prayer I believe I have been able to live the life I have. Also, I have a list of close friends who need to be contacted. I would like to visit with them before I pass away. I do not want my ex-wives' contact. I do not believe they would care anyway."

When the patient met with the pastor, he again verbalized not having a fear of death. However, he did have a great curiosity about what happens once one dies. He told the pastor, "Even after all the people I cared for died, it bothered me. The dying did not bother me, but some of those people who underwent that scared me. I mean people who were violent and who killed and stabbed other people—murderers and rapists. I believe down deep I know where they went. I believe in God and life after death, but at times my faith is weak, and I have doubts." The pastor told the patient, "Tell God what is going on in your mind. Ask him for his grace through Jesus." The pastor prayed with the patient. Afterward, the patient wept. He said, "I have not cried like this since my father and mother passed away. You see, my father disowned me because I would not come back and take over the farm. Because of the differences we had, I did not get to tell him I loved him and missed him before he passed away. My father's pastor told me my father had told him after several years he missed me too. Also, I should have not condemned my son for not taking over the farm. I let my anger destroy my relationship with my son."

On the fifth night, after being admitted into the hospice inpatient unit, the patient said, "I had an out-of-body experience. I was in that tunnel with light, which people always talk about. The light was so inviting. It pulled me into a beautiful valley. Suddenly I felt at ease and at peace. My father showed up and looked like a young man. He had a glow about him, and he was in perfect health. He told me, 'When you arrive, you will have eternity to grow in the light of the Lord. Your mother, grandparents, and old friends will be waiting to see you. With your kind heart and willingness to care for people, you'll feel right at home. You'll have to go back for a few days, and then you will pass away.'"

For the last three days, the patient was in and out of consciousness. At times he was awake and alert. He spent time with his sister, his niece, and nephew, and old friends.

At his funeral, a close friend spoke and said he was a kind man. She said, "As we celebrate his life, we remember he cared for thousands of people with kindness and love. If ever there was an angel born on earth, it would be him. I will always remember his positive attitude even on the darkest days."

The hospice nurse reminded the sister and friends of the yearly hospice remembrance. Also, if any of them needed to talk and speak with one of the social workers or pastors feel free to do so at any time. Counseling for the family and friends after the patient has passed away is part of the hospice benefit.

The End

Gratitude

THE PATIENT WAS a forty-seven-year-old person with a diagnosis of advanced cancer of the brain. Clinical findings exhibit widespread metastatic disease. His doctor told him, "I'm sorry I have to tell you this, but you have very little time left." With your permission, I will refer you to hospice care services. The patient said, "I can feel my life slipping away from me. I do agree. However, hospice care now will be my best option. My father always told me, 'Two things will always happen to you, son. You're born and then you die.' It is still very shocking to learn this, and I appreciate the fact that you told me upfront. My family will be devastated. My wife, children, and grand-children had expressed their fear this might happen."

The patient was contacted by the hospice nurse who set up an appointment. When she met the patient and his wife, the wife was in complete denial. She said, "I don't like the sound of hospice. It scares the hell out of me. You are going to give him a bunch of drugs and knock him off." The hospice nurse instructed the patient and his wife on hospice in the grieving process. She told the patient's wife, "We will only use enough medication to keep him comfortable. We will use low-dose liquid morphine for pain. The rule of thumb is to start low and go slow. We are not like Dr. Kevorkian. We don't start IVs in both arms and medicate somebody to exterminate them. That is not what hospice is all about. We just keep people comfortable manage their symptoms of dying as shortness of breath pain and restlessness and support the family. We have medications for restlessness so he can remain calm. Medication for pain so he will be kept comfortable and slowly pass away in peace with his family at his side. Also, this will allow you and the family to spend quality time with him and celebrate the time you have left with him.

"The other benefits of hospice that will be provided are a social worker to assist you with mortuary and funeral arrangements if needed. The social worker can also research other benefits you might qualify for. Also, very good at contacting people for you and counseling family members who are grieving. A nurse aide will provide bathing and light housekeeping. I will authorize three times a week to start. As you progress, I will change that to daily.

"The last benefit is a hospice pastor if you request one. I can assign one, and he can also make regular visits." The patient said, "I would like to have a hospice pastor visit. My wife is a Catholic and I am a Baptist. However, that never stopped us from living a good life and raising our children. I am familiar with hospice. I have had a few close friends who I helped care for when they were passing away in hospice."

The nurse said, "If you like, we have a social worker who is very experienced in counseling and working with teenagers. It truly would make things easier for your kids." The patient's wife said, "I just don't understand why he has to die now. He's too young, and it's not fair."

Again, the nurse reviewed the dying process with the patient's wife. She remained in denial, and the nurse documented this and decided to call and speak privately with the social worker and pastor and report on the patient, especially his wife's denial. She will need counseling from the pastor and social worker. Also, the nurse asked the patient to "Call the wife's priest so he could speak to her and assist her in her denial and grief also." The patient said, "I will do that after you leave. That is a good idea. She really likes Father Lopez. So I'll make sure he's the one I speak to." The children at that time appeared to understand the process more than the wife. This will be reported to the social worker also.

The next day the social worker and pastor visited the patient and his wife together. After their visit, the hospice nurse case manager visited also. She was there for twenty minutes, and the nurse aide showed up to give the patient a bath. After his bath, the patient said, "I should've had people bathing me all my life this was great." The patient's wife said, "He has always required extra attention. I always gave it to him because I love him so much. After meeting with the pastor and the social worker, I believe I am starting to grasp hospice palliative care in a way I did not understand before."

The wife continued, "Father Lopez called me after you know who called him. He said, 'Your husband wanted me to speak to you about his disease, and the time he has left is very short.' We spoke for an hour and one half. I realize now I was in denial. It was more anger than anything. This will be hard for me because we have known each other since the fifth grade in elementary school. I fell in love with him then and have loved him ever since."

For thirty days, the patient continued to slowly decline and become totally bedbound. He was becoming forgetful and having periods of confusion. Also, he would go in and out of consciousness. His moments of clarity were short. The patient's wife said, "I feel like this is getting to be too much to handle." The nurse case manager asked the patient's wife if she would like to put him in an inpatient unit. "We could set up a cot for you in his room. You could sleep in his room with him at night if you choose. Or you can go home and rest at night. If anything were to happen during the night, you would be called immediately." The nurse called and received orders to admit the patient to the hospice inpatient unit. The nurse then called and arrange transport for the patient to the unit.

On the first night in the inpatient unit, the patient had a period of two hours of being alert and oriented; his clarity was normal. He thanked his wife for the love and the life he had with her and also for their beautiful children. They both reminisced about the time they first met in different events in their lives. The first time they ever kissed was in the sixth grade. The patient's wife said, "It took him a year to get up the courage to kiss me in the sixth grade." The patient said, "When we did kiss, I believe I knew then for sure I was totally in love with her. Isn't that wild? It was not puppy love." The patient's wife said, "I know you loved me, and I loved you. It was from the first time we sat next to each other in class, in the fifth grade."

On the first night in the inpatient unit, the patient's wife slept in a cot next to his bed. In the morning she told the nurse, "I had a beautiful dream last night. An angel came and pulled my soul out of my body and took me where my husband would go when he passes. Everything that seemed enhanced in the colors was phenomenal. I just don't know how to describe how beautiful they were: the vivid landscape and the color of the sky, and it was like you were part of it and could feel its beauty. The angel told me my husband would be greeted by several people in his life who have passed away. People he knew briefly whom he liked. So he will be surprised to see those people whom he briefly knew, deceased family members. Dear old friends are waiting to see him and see the light of the spirit in his continued covenant with God through Jesus Christ."

The patient passed away two days later with his family at his side. At least ninety people attended his funeral services. The social worker reminded the wife that every year hospice has a one-year remembrance for people who had passed away the previous year. She told the wife, "You will be notified by mail if you want to attend. You're not obligated to do this. Only if you wish to. There'll be other families there remembering their family members who have passed also."

At the one-year remembrance, the patient's wife and children attended the remembrance, especially the children. They learned what the celebration of life is all about. The patient's wife said, "God sent all the right people to help us through our grief and my denial at the right time. We cannot express our gratitude for everything. Thank you very much."

The End

Food for Angels

THE PATIENT WAS admitted to hospice care with a diagnosis of terminal lung cancer. Clinical findings exhibited malignancy with aggressive metastatic disease. He had a decrease in performance status and significant unintentional weight loss. He had refused any lifesaving medical treatment. His family doctor referred him over to hospice care, which was to be followed by the hospice medical director.

The patient was a seventy-five-year-old widower. His spouse passed away in her early fifties. He never had any children but has nieces and nephews and many dear friends. He lived a very full life cooking food and serving others. The patient said, "I have been a cook all my life. I did not have any formal training. I started cooking as a child with my mother. Everybody in my family loved the food I would cook. At an early age, I opened my own family restaurant. I funded it from the life insurance policy my mother left me when she passed away. I hired and trained all my own staff to be respectful and courteous to our customers."

The hospice nurse who admitted the patient explained all the hospice services to him. He also explained the pain control he would be receiving—medication for any signs or symptoms of anxiety and restlessness. He would be receiving a nurse aide to bathe him and do some light housekeeping and a social worker to assist him with any personal needs such as mortuary and funeral arrangements and to assist with contacting people for him and other community services available to him.

The patient has a close friend with him who also had his power of attorney. He was in the patient's church group and volunteered to stay with him at home until he would pass away. He said, "I already have funeral arrangements in place. My pastor from my church will do my eulogy. When my power of attorney needs a break, someone from our church will come and stay with me when he is out." The nurse arranged an in-service with the patient's power of attorney and his friends from church to make sure appropriate palliative care measures were followed. He reinforced the safe administration of liquid morphine. Also, safe administration of his antianxiety medication. "The anxiety medication is called Ativan. The morphine and Ativan are both liquids and instructions are on the bottles. Do not deviate from the instructions on these bottles. Every time a dose is given, write it down on the flow sheets. This way when I come to make a visit, I can assess how effective the medication is working."

The social worker contacted the patient's nieces and nephews and spoke with them. They were instructed on hospice services and were told that counseling services will be available to them to help them through the grieving process of death and dying. The patient said, "I have outlived all my family and my generation. My brother and sister never educated my nieces and nephews on the importance of family. I never missed a birthday or graduation with these kids. They refused to come and see me, and it hurts me deeply. Everything I have will be split between my closest friends in my church. They're the ones who have been by my side and loved me all these years."

On admission patient's pain was 8 on a 0–10 pain scale with 10 being the highest level of pain. The low doses of liquid morphine were given consistently by his friends acting as his caregivers and documented. In two days, the patient's pain level decreased from an 8 to a 2 on the pain scale. He did become restless, and Ativan was given to him every four hours as ordered.

His pastor from his church made daily visits to the patient. They talked about old times and prayed. Also, other church members came and held prayer sessions with him.

On the eighth night of his second month in hospice home care, he started talking openly to an angel with his eyes shut. He verbalized, "This tunnel has the most beautiful lighting. Where am I and who are you? You look like an old friend from long ago. You are much younger than he was." This person said, "I am one of your old friends. I have come to show you where you will be going on the next part of your spiritual journey. Jesus has prepared the way for you. All is well. Love is life." The patient said, "You have a beautiful glow about you very peaceful."

"I am your angel. Remember twenty years ago you helped a down-and-out bum. You took me off the street and nursed me back to health. You gave me a bus ticket to get back home. I got back home, and my brother got me a good job. I worked for that company for the rest of my life. I raised a family and had two children. I always told them about the nice man who pulled me from the pit and helped me get home. Now I will help you receive the grace that Christ has prepared for you from the father."

The next evening the patient passed away. At his funeral between old friends and church friends, four hundred people showed up. They all agreed he was a very nice man. He fed his customers; he fed the sick and homeless at his restaurant. The pastor said, "The patient said it won't be long, and I will be cooking for angels."

The patient's death was very peaceful, and everyone believed he went to heaven. On the yearly remembrance book by the hospice, over ninety people showed up just to remember him. The pastor said, "He is up there cooking. That's all he ever wanted to do was feed people."

The End

The Recruiter

THE PATIENT WAS admitted to hospice home care with the diagnosis of recurrent congestive heart failure at rest with refractory angina and also the inability to carry out physical activities without discomfort and symptoms of heart failure at rest with increased discomfort with minimal exertion.

The hospice nurse explained services to the patient and her daughter. The patient was told, "You will be on a morphine liquid for pain, and we will continue your regular medications especially your nitroglycerin patches for your heart. You will continue with oxygen, and we will set up a suction machine and teach your daughter how to use it." The nurse asked the daughter, "Are you willing to learn how to use the suction machine?" The daughter said, "I am a nurse aide, and I have used a suction machine before in emergencies until an RN came and took over. So I have no problem suctioning my mother if needed."

The nurse asked the patient and daughter, "When you get closer to passing, do you want to stay at home or be admitted to the hospice inpatient unit? At the unit, your daughter can stay with you and sleep in a cot. You both will be provided your meals, and you would have twenty-four-hour nursing care around the clock." The patient said, "That's up to my daughter. She knows what she could handle and not." The daughter said, "I think when she gets close the unit would be a good idea. I could spend more quality time with her before she goes into a coma. I know how this works I have seen it before."

The nurse said, "I will get an order from your doctor to do this so we don't have to get orders at the last minute. The other services we will provide as your daughter knows will be a nurse aide for bathing starting out three times a week. As you progress, I will increase that to daily as ordered by the physician. A social worker will come to visit you and assist you with any mortuary and funeral arrangements. Also, the social workers are very good at counseling and finding other services in the community that you may utilize. Do you have a priest or pastor you want us to contact, or would you prefer the hospice pastor? Even if you have your priest or pastor come to make visits, our hospice pastor can also if you want."

The patient said, "My funeral arrangements are already made, and I paid for my plot. The mortuary said they could provide a pastor if needed. I would prefer to have a hospice pastor do the eulogy that has worked with me." The daughter said, "I agree. I've met some hospice pastors, and they're great."

On admission, the patient's pain was a nine on the 0–10 pain scale. The patient and the daughter were instructed on the dosage of liquid morphine. Her daughter was very capable of assisting her mother with this appropriately. Within twenty-four hours, her pain decreased to a 4. At forty-eight hours, her pain level decreased to a 2 on the pain scale. She continued with all her regular medications. At this point, she was sitting up in bed eating and talking with her daughter and friends who were visiting. The patient said, "It's nice to be out of pain. I can't believe how good I feel right now." The nurse told the patient, "This was our goal—to get you as comfortable as possible and that you have a quality of life as you pass."

By the fifth day, the patient was in total care. She and her daughter requested that she be admitted into the hospice inpatient unit. The patient said, "I am suddenly very anxious and fear death." The nurse said, "I will let the pastor know you're going to the unit. So the pastor can see you there, and I will make sure that's today."

Once in the hospice inpatient unit, the patient appeared to be less stressed out. Having professional nursing care twenty-four hours a day always makes a great difference. Also, it will assist the patient's daughter and her grieving process. The patient got to where her fluid intake was low, but her mouth was dry. Swabs were provided that would moisten her lips and mouth, also ice chips. Her daughter would only leave her side to go home clean up and shower.

The patient prayed with the pastor and her daughter. This relaxed her when she was restless. Also, a low dose of Ativan a benzodiazepine was started to help her relax.

The nurse asked the patient, "What has your greatest happiness in life been?" She said, "Believing in Christ as my Lord and Savior. Also, I had a very active life in sales. I sold high-end jewelry and was very good at it. However, for the last ten years—well, almost ten years—I was a recruiter for an agency. We recruited CPAs, accountants, and mostly clerical staff. I was just as good at that as I was at sales. All my friends said that I was relentless. If I get to go to heaven I would like to recruit for God. I will be relentless for our Lord and Savior and father above."

Four days later in the morning, the patient woke up and said, "I had a vision last night, and Saint Peter came to visit me and tell me I would have a job as a recruiter for God. Also, I would have to wait three days to go." The nurse asked the patient, "What did Saint Peter look like?" The patient said, "He was average height and not bad looking. Also, he looked illuminated and comforting. He did that thing, you know the life review, and I passed. In sales, I did most of my life I never compromised my integrity. I mean the jewelry that I sold to people was quality. I never compromised or lied to anybody about what they were buying. I told the truth always. He told me my greatest quality was honesty. 'You are relentless like people have told you but in a good way. And you always prayed and asked forgiveness for your sins.' Just now I woke up.

"I forgot also Saint Peter said, 'It will be three days until your angel comes to take you. Your angel will be a surprise. However, she will help train and orient you to your new eternal life, and you'll start the job requested.' I told him, 'This is exciting. I can't wait to get started.' I have to tell you heaven is beautiful. The panorama takes your breath away."

That evening the patient passed away, with her daughter, the hospice pastor, and inpatient staff at her side. The nurse reported static electricity in the room and a rush of warm air out of nowhere that lasted about five seconds. The pastor said, "That was her spirit passing through us on her way to be with the Lord."

The End

My Heart, My Love

THE PATIENT WAS a ninety-year-old male who lived alone. His admitting diagnosis to hospice palliative care was end-stage heart failure. He had been noncompliant with his medications. In the last six months, he had gone into congestive heart failure four times. The fourth time, response was poor to optimal treatment with diuretics and vasodilators. He now had congestive heart failure at rest with refractory angina, inability to carry out physical activities without discomfort, and symptoms of heart failure at rest with increased discomfort even with minimal exertion.

The patient's spouse passed away approximately a year ago. Since she passed, he mentally had given up. He was not ready for his wife's passing. She just passed away in her sleep, and he could not wake her up in the morning. According to a close friend after the funeral, he said, "Now that my love is gone, I want to die so I can be in heaven with her. We were married for seventy-two years." His neighbor said, "They went to grade school together, high school, and college together. They had no children and attended their church and donated to causes and their community. For the last fifteen years, he has been volunteering at the senior center close to our homes. He has outlived all his family and now his only family is his church family."

The patient was referred to a hospice inpatient unit by his primary doctor. His primary doctor also requested that the hospice medical director follow the patient. The medical director accepted the patient and admitted him to the inpatient unit for hospice palliative care.

Once on the unit, the admitting nurse explained hospice services to the patient. The registered nurse and nurse aide gave him a bed bath and cleaned him from head to toe. He had not had a bath for a while. After his bath, he slept for six hours straight. When he woke up, the nurse asked the patient, "Do you have any special friends you want us to contact?" He said, "My neighbor and my pastor. My neighbor knows I'm here, and he's going to tell our pastor." The nurse asked the patient, "Do you have any mortuary and funeral arrangements made?"

"Yes," he said, "I purchased the plot right next to my wife, and the services are already prepaid for at the mortuary." So as not to violate this patient's right to privacy, we did not list the name of the mortuary. The nurse reported the phone number of the patient's neighbor and his pastor's number. The social worker arrived at the unit. He passed on this information he had just received to the social worker. The social worker then connected with the friend and the pastor. They both would come that day to visit the patient.

That evening, the patient told the nurse, "When I was young, they would not allow me to join the marines, army, and air force. They told me I had a heart murmur, and I should go to college and get a career without any physical demands because of my heart. As it ended up, I went to the same college as my wife, and we got married at eighteen years old. I became a certified public accountant. My wife became a registered nurse. I believe I lasted all these years because she always made sure I did everything I needed to do to care for my heart. I miss her so bad that it hurts. We grew up in the same neighborhood, and we walked to school from grade school through high school until I was able to drive. Then I drove her to school every day also. I believe we knew we loved each other then. We were waiting for the appropriate time. It was different than we lived by high morals and standards. I realized when I was thirty years old, she was forever my heart, my love."

The patient continued, "In my sleep, my sweetheart came to me last night. It was so real it did not feel like a dream. She told me tomorrow we will be together for eternity. I asked her, 'Is this for sure? Will it be tomorrow?' And she said yes. I did not see any tunnels or bright lights like people say. She was just there like in a picture talking to me. I called my pastor and told him what she said. He said, 'I will be there at noon to visit and pray with you. If you go tonight, you will be with her again. I believe she came to prepare the way for you so you would not be afraid.'" The pastor and the patient had a good visit and prayed at noon. At 4 p.m., the patient passed away.

As the nurse was cleaning up the patient's room after he passed. He found a stationary card. It was pink and with very beautiful handwriting it said, "My love, my heart."

The patient passed away in peace; he was a kind gentleman who was always willing to lend a hand to others. His church pastor said, "He loved volunteering at the senior center. He delivered Meals on Wheels voluntarily for several years also. He loved interpersonal communication with people. He would always pray with people. He truly was one of God's children."

At a very young age, that patient took Christ into his heart. He admitted he had sinned at times and had doubts. In the end, he knew where he was going. Now he truly is with his only true love.

The End

Back to Life

THE PATIENT WAS admitted to hospice home care for advanced end-stage senescence. For the past six months, she had gone from 120 pounds to 78 pounds; the patient had lost greater than 10 percent of her body mass. Also, she had declining albumin. In addition to this, she had the inability to maintain sufficient fluid and caloric intake. She said, "I just have no appetite, and when I go to drink something, it feels like I'm choking."

When the hospice registered nurse was assessing the patient, the patient had been doctor shopping for over a year. She was on multiple medications—a gross number of medications. She had seven doctors writing prescriptions for her. The nurse asked the patient and her husband if it would be okay for the hospice medical director to follow her. They asked why.

The nurse asked the patient, "Have the seven doctors been communicating with each other?" The patient said, "I don't know. I don't believe so." The husband said, "No, I don't think they are communicating with each other. I don't read stuff that comes in the mail or talk to her doctors. I am legally blind. I use this magnifier to set up her med sets just as all the medications are ordered by all these doctors. I thought they were just trying to save her, and it wasn't working. Her last doctor made the hospice referral."

The patient said, "Do you think I have been taking too much medication?" The nurse said, "That's what I'm thinking. The medical director would come out and assess you in your home. Then we would develop together a plan of care to keep you comfortable. Tell me. did you want hospice?" The patient said, "I figured it would be best since I'm dying, and I can't hold anything down."

"Well," the nurse said, "maybe it's a long shot, but it's worth a try with the medical director. What do you think?" The patient said, "Yes, I want to do this. I want the medical director."

The nurse contacted the medical director and reported her findings from the assessment. She told the medical director about her conversation with the patient and her spouse. The medical director said, "Tell them I will be there at 2 p.m., and let's get to the bottom of everything and really help this lady one way or the other."

The nurse explained hospice services to the patient and her spouse. Also, she would come back after the medical director had made his assessment. She said, "I want to wait and see what type of medications the medical director will order. Do you have any pain?" The patient said, "I have very little pain, but I do have a lot of anxiety over taking all these pills." The nurse said, "Well, the medical director is a good man. He will help you straighten everything out. I promise."

The medical director spent an hour and a half with the patient, assessing her and speaking to her and her husband in detail. He also called all the doctors who had written prescriptions to find out any history of the patient they knew.

The medical director ordered medications to increase the patient's appetite and also medication to relieve her choking symptoms. He also diagnosed that the patient was overmedicated. In addition to this, her spouse who was legally blind was setting up her med sets wrong. He determined it wouldn't have mattered secondary to her taking all the medications she did not need.

The hospice nurse visited with the patient and her spouse the next day, reviewed all the medical director's orders, and wrote a care plan for the patient. She also had her medications filled by the pharmacy the hospice used. They were filled into med sets with the appropriate times.

Three months later, the medical director discharged the patient from hospice. She had gained a total of thirty-one pounds. She was ambulating without assistance and was able to tolerate food and fluids without signs and symptoms of aspiration. On the day of discharge, the patient drove to the store and went shopping.

The patient was extremely grateful. She said, "Back to life." She was a sweet lady and ready to continue her life's journey with her husband.

The End

Conscious Contact and Connection with God

THE PATIENT WAS admitted to hospice home care with a diagnosis of terminal lung cancer and clinical findings of malignancy—widespread aggressive metastatic disease. In addition to this, he had heart disease and congestive heart failure, poor response to treatment with diuretics and vasodilators, inability to carry out physical activities without discomfort, and heart failure and increased discomfort with minimal exertion. The patient requested hospice home care for comfort measures.

The patient was well-known to criminals. He was a prosecutor who never lost a case. He said, "I cannot believe at my age, I am at the end of my life. I had so many plans for retirement. One must face reality. I never married because I didn't want a wife or children to be a target for criminals. I prosecuted criminals who were the worst morally in our society. To this day I still receive personal threats on my life. However, it looks like cancer and heart disease are doing the job for the people who want to kill me."

The hospice nurse explained the services to the patient. The patient refused social services. He did require a nurse aide and the patient agreed to the nurse aide. The patient said, "I have made arrangements with the mortuary for a burial plot. All the things I will need after I'm gone are taken care of. They are in place ready to go."

The patient was a Catholic and had a long relationship with his priest. He attended mass three to five times a week for most of his life. His priest had already confirmed he will visit the patient daily. He had already performed the last rites. The nurse spoke with the priest, and the priest said, "The patient has had over one hundred death threats from people he has prosecuted. I cannot count the times he was under protective custody himself. One time he was shot at getting in his car. It turned out to be a person he had helped convict several years earlier who was out on parole. He has lived a very exciting and full life."

The patient had several close friends whom he had worked with staying with him and providing care until he passes. In addition to this, he was visited by several high-ranking state officials and other community leaders. Throughout his life, he received many awards for standing up for justice.

The patient verbalized he was more comfortable with hospice symptom management. He was receiving liquid morphine that helped with his chest pain and breathing. He also had nitroglycerin patches that helped with his chest pain also.

As the patient progressed, he started having visions. He said, "I believe I am having visions, not dreams. I should read up on how to classify this. In my vision, my mother tells me how proud she is of me and the work I did for society. However, my father consistently told me I should practice a different type of law. 'You should find a good Catholic girl, get married, and have children.' In the vision when he spoke to me, he had changed. He said, 'You did a very unselfish thing by not having a family. You served your community and your country with honor.' Also, the dog I had growing up was in the vision. He was eleven years old when he passed away. In the vision, he was young and healthy and brought me the frisbee to throw for him. That dog reminded me of friendship and unconditional love."

The patient continued, "I'm a little freaked out. All the visions are so vivid and seem so real." The nurse said, "The visits you are having are people who love you very much. I believe they are preparing the way for you. It's one of the promises that Jesus made to us. He died for our sins to prepare the way for us. How awesome is that? Christ sent you this vision to reduce your fears of death that he knows you have. Your transition is in motion. Congratulations!"

The patient said, "I have always believed in God and accepted Christ as my Lord and Savior when I was sixteen years old, even though I had been baptized as an infant. I made a covenant to always try to be the best person I could be. I learned the Ten Commandments that I had to repeat to my father every night until I had them down perfectly. At times I have had my doubts, and I asked for forgiveness for this. I believe I decreased the doubts by attending church regularly and maintaining a conscious contact and connection with God, you know that connection with God through prayer."

Five days after the patient's visions, he said, "I was floating outside my body last night. This beautiful lady told me when I was floating, 'You will pass away tonight. Prepare to be visited and be with family and old friends tonight.'

"She then showed me vivid colorful landscapes and the beauty in heaven. She said, 'Life after mortal death is beautiful. You will be healthy and be able to do all the things that are good and righteous you ever wanted to do and did not have time to do.' I have to say that the colors everywhere were just so impressive like a different dimension. I know I sound like I'm crazy. Well, if I am, it's very exciting."

That evening with old friends, his priest, and the hospice nurse at his bedside, the patient passed away peacefully.

At his funeral, his priest performed his eulogy. He said, "In the Old Testament, God said, 'An eye for an eye and a tooth for a tooth.' What he meant was to seek equal justice. Our dear brother in Christ believed that justice was part of our covenant with God. He was a good man who sacrificed his life for the good of society. He fought hard and sacrificed all his life to protect all of us unselfishly. God bless him, and may he rest in peace."

The End

It's Not Supposed to Be Easy

THE PATIENT WAS an elderly male with a diagnosis of heart failure at rest, refractory angina, inability to carry out physical activities without discomfort, symptoms of angina at rest, and increased discomfort with minimal exertion.

The patient lived with his daughter and son-in-law. They had cared for him for the last nine years. The patient requested hospice care, and his daughter honored his wishes. His primary doctor agreed and made the hospice referral. He also wrote an order for the hospice medical director to assume care for the patient.

The nurse instructed the patient, his daughter, and his son-in-law on hospice services. He would be receiving liquid morphine for pain. Ativan is a benzodiazepine, which is an antianxiety drug for anxiety and restlessness. The daughter refused a social worker. However, she did agree to have a hospice pastor visit with the patient. In addition to this, a nurse aide would come three times a week for bathing.

The patient remained on oxygen and had his own oxygenator for the house. Also, the patient and family agreed to have a hospice volunteer visit for companionship with the patient. Again, the hospice registered nurse reiterated all the services available from hospice. This patient already had his own hospital bed and all the equipment. The nurse reviewed the symptom management of the dying again with the daughter and son-in-law. "The morphine liquid to be used will be started at a low dose. You will be using a liquid dropper, and all you have to do is squeeze it into his mouth. We start morphine at a low dose and titrate up to the level the patient is most comfortable with without putting him in a coma. Also, I will be visiting daily for the first week. If you feel you need me day or night or just want to talk, call our office, and they will relay the message to me, and I will contact you."

The hospice pastor met with the patient the next day. The patient said, "I went to church every Sunday most of my life, except when I had to work. I have not gone for at least six months. It has really brought me down not being able to go. For years going to church for me was like refueling my spirit. It could have been a terrible week then I would walk out of church at the end of the services always feeling like a new man. I am very lucky. My daughter and son-in-law have taken good care of me, and shortly I will not be a burden to them anymore. I remember I asked God why things always have to be so damn hard. I know this sounds crazy, but a voice in both my ears told me it's not supposed to be easy. After that I thought, *Man, now, I am really going crazy. Voices are talking to me.* Then I realized it was probably God telling me even though things are damn hard, I can get through it. I have taken comfort in that. I mean what else can I do? God is in charge, and that's just the way it is."

The patient continued, "My wife passed away eighteen years ago. I believe it was love at first sight, and she was very easy to talk to about anything. I met her at church. It took me six months to get the courage to ask her on a date. I finally asked her out, and she said yes. We were engaged for two years then we married. We had our daughter who is so precious to me and takes care of me now. I think being around her these years are the only thing that kept me alive. She knows how much I loved her mother and how much losing her really hurt me. At first, I was angry with her for leaving me. It's not like she left me for another man. She just went to sleep one night and never woke up. The Next morning, I found her stiff and cold. I think it haunts me. I always thought I would go first. Good things are around the corner I can feel it.

"Last night that voice spoke to me again. It said, 'You will die in two days.' I told the voice I'm ready to go and be with my beloved wife. The voice said, 'All these years, there are times you complained about how hard things are, but you always prayed to God for solutions. The times that you did not get what you prayed for, it was only

God saying no. You have lived a clean life. You worshiped the father through Christ all these years.'"

Two days later the patient passed away. His daughter, son-in-law, hospice pastor, and nurse were at the bedside. The hospice pastor said a prayer as they all held hands. The daughter cried and said, "I will miss you, Papa. I love you, but now you can be with Mama. God bless you."

The patient's daughter continued, "He was such a kind and gentle man. When I was a little girl, every Friday night, he would take me to Dairy Queen. I remember once he was very sick. It was a Friday, and I asked him 'Are we going to Dairy Queen tonight, Papa?' My mother said, 'You can't go tonight because your papa is sick.' I started to walk out of the room, and my papa was up out of bed and getting dressed. He said, 'Nothing makes you feel better when you're sick than Dairy Queen.' It wasn't till years later my mother told me, 'You were so preoccupied and getting your ice cream you didn't notice Papa didn't get anything. By you getting that ice cream actually did make him feel better. He loved you so much he just wanted to keep you happy and that made him happy.'"

At his funeral, the hospice pastor gave his eulogy. "The patient was a family man. He lost his wife eighteen years ago and never truly got over it. He is survived by his loving daughter and son-in-law. He was the kind of man who always gave to others. He got joy out of helping others. In these times today, we need more people like him. May he rest in peace and in God's loving arms."

The nurse reminded the daughter and son-in-law about the one-year remembrance that hospice has for all the patients who had passed away previously. She asked, "Do you want to be contacted for the remembrance? There is no obligation to do this only if you want to." The daughter said, "No, we will remember him well. I will honor him and put flowers on his grave along with my mother's. Well, maybe I might come. I'm just...well, all this grief...I wouldn't want to start it up again."

The End

She Was a Kind, Loving Mother

THE PATIENT WAS an eighty-year-old female admitted to the hospice inpatient unit with diagnosis of end-stage renal disease, type II diabetes mellitus, chronic obstructive pulmonary disease, and a history of manic depression. She was currently depressed and angry. Her primary doctor said she would be okay if she would not refuse dialysis. Her daughter who had her medical power of attorney was also refusing dialysis for her mother. So her primary doctor, nephrologist, pulmonologist, and psychiatrist all agreed it was time for hospice.

The patient had 3+ edema in her extremities. She was refusing any food or fluids. She will be kept comfortable as possible. Medication for pain and medication for restlessness and anxiety. Any of her other medications will be continued as a comfort measure.

On admission to the hospice inpatient unit, the patient was a DNR (do not resuscitate). After the nurse instructed her and her daughter and the services she would be receiving, she passed away!

She should have been referred to hospice much earlier. This does happen a lot. And it was not the doctor's fault. The patient and family hesitate or someone in the family is in complete denial. It's rare that the patient is in denial. It's usually one or all the family members. This patient had a small family. I cannot imagine the stress her daughter had been under all this time caring for her mother.

The social worker on the unit sat down with her daughter and helped to arrange mortuary and funeral arrangements. Her mother was to be cremated, and she will have a small ceremony with old friends. The hospice pastor will give the eulogy.

At the ceremony, the pastor spoke about the patient from information he received from the daughter. He said, "When she was young, she went to college and became a registered nurse. She became a psych nurse. She had the insight to help people because of her own disease. At fifty years old, her disease took over. She could no longer work and went on disability." She was survived by her daughter who said, "All the friends here knew her well. She truly was a kind woman, and her goal was to always help people who had the problem she had. But she declined quickly with other physical problems. She was a good Christian and had taken Christ into her heart when she was a young woman. She was a kind and loving mother, and I will miss her always." The pastor said, "The Lord giveth and the Lord taketh away. Blessed be the word of the Lord. After all, she went through, he took it early so she wouldn't suffer anymore. We will miss her, and God bless her."

The End

I Love Her with All My Heart

THE PATIENT WAS a twenty-nine-year-old female admitted to the hospice palliative care inpatient unit with diagnosis of HIV disease and noncompliance with her HIV meds. She was bedbound and required assistance with all essentials of daily living. Her weight loss was greater than 33 percent of lean body mass. She had renal failure in the absence of dialysis. She had advanced HIV disease to the extent that it indicated hospice care.

The patient had sex with a young man when she went to college. He infected her with HIV. They did not practice safe sex. The young man passed away a year ago apparently; he infected several young women. The patient had consistently refused lifesaving measures. She said, "I refuse to live a life hooked up to a dialysis machine three times a week. I'm not a candidate for a kidney transplant. I just want to be cared for and kept comfortable until I die."

After the physical assessment, the RN explained the services she would be receiving in the hospice inpatient unit. Her doctor signed the standard palliative care orders for pain, restlessness, and anxiety. It also includes bowel care and any of her regular meds that would assist in keeping her comfortable. A certified nursing assistant will visit with her every shift to provide bowel and urinary care, also a bath if needed. The social worker will assist her with mortuary and funeral arrangements. A hospice pastor will assist her with her spiritual needs.

Once admitted the medical director of the hospice requested to take over her care from her primary doctor who agreed. Also, the patient agreed to this change in physician.

The patient said, "I do not have anyone at home to care for me anymore. I have been abandoned by my friends and family because of HIV. I would like to see the pastor, and the social worker as soon as possible. I want to see if my mother and father would come to see me." The social worker met with the patient first. He called and spoke with the patient's father and mother by phone. The mother and the patient's other siblings refused to come to see her. However, her father said, "I will go see her and spend time with her. She is my oldest child, and I will not let her die alone. I've always been proud of her even after she made some very bad decisions. She became a pharmacist and for years helped lots of people with their pharmaceutical needs. You see I love her with all my heart and always will."

The patient met with the pastor and asked the pastor to help her pray that her family would come and visit her. After they finished, the social worker came in. The social worker told the patient, "Your father would be coming to visit you, and he will stay with you until the end. Also, the hospice foundation agreed to pay your mortuary and funeral expenses." The patient was elated!

The patient graduated from college as a pharmacist. She had worked six days a week for years. She said, "I know it sounds bad since I'm a pharmacist, and I was noncompliant with my HIV meds. Now I have renal failure on top of it. I just cannot do it anymore. After I had been infected, I never had sex again. Well, it's been ten years since I was infected, and everything has been downhill since then. I worked hard as a pharmacist, stuck to myself, and never had gotten close two anybody again after being abandoned by my friends in college.

"The man who infected me, we had dated for five months. I finally gave in and had sex with him. I did not use safe sex. He did not wear a prophylactic. I told him it would be okay because I was on the pill. Also, for the last six months, I pretty much have only taken my medications on and off. By doing that, my body started to break down, and a lot of other things happen to it. I have been feeling very guilty for a long time. I know I am at the end of it, and I just want to die free of pain.

"My family had disowned me and treated me like the plague. It was because of most of my mother's ideology. Now that I know my father's coming to see and be with me. It confirms to me that it was mostly my mother. And she turned the rest of my family against me. I always loved them and treated them well.

"The only people who have been kind to me have been doctors, nurses, social workers, and pastors. Without these special people, I would not have made it this far. However, as I meet the end of this life, I just want to be with the Lord. I know I let my family down. I have apologized, but they treat me like I never existed."

The nurse reviewed the hospice medications with the patient. She would be receiving liquid morphine starting at a low dose and titrated up to her level of comfort, in addition to this, a benzodiazepine called Ativan for anxiety and restlessness. The patient said, "I know all about those medications. I'm a pharmacist." The nurse laughed and said, "You probably know more about the medications than I do chemically and their interactions." The nurse then asked the patient, "On a 0–10 pain scale, what would you say your pain is now?" The patient said, "It's a 7 on the scale." The nurse administered the first dose of liquid morphine.

That afternoon the patient's father showed up at the hospice inpatient unit. He requested a cot and planned on staying with the patient until she passes. When the patient saw her father, she cried and so did he. He hugged her and said, "I had a dream about the two of us spending time together until the end. Also, recently I got baptized and accepted Christ as my Lord and Savior. I took him into my heart. I feel like a new man. You know, dear, I always have loved you with all my heart."

The father then asked the patient to get baptized. She agreed and the nurse spoke to the pastor and told him what the patient wanted to do. She also told him that the father was going to be with the patient until she would pass. And he had told her he had recently been baptized. The hospice pastor baptized her; she accepted Christ into her heart. Then the pastor presented her with a certificate of baptism. The patient gave the certificate to her father and said, "I want you to keep this as a remembrance of me, Dad." Her father broke down and cried. He said, "Now you will be in the arms of our Lord for eternity."

That night around midnight, the patient woke up and told her father, "I had a dream an angel came to me. He told me I would be going to heaven and the Lord had forgiven all my sins and deep down, I was really a good person and will have eternity to live in the light of the Lord."

The next day the patient and her father spent time reminiscing about the past and her childhood—the special moments they spent together as she was growing up. Her father told her how proud he was of her for becoming a pharmacist and helping so many people. Her father told her, "That dream you say you had was not a dream. It was a vision to help you lower your fears about the unknown."

Two days later the patient passed away with her father at her side. At her funeral, only a few friends showed up, and her father did. Her mother and siblings declined to go.

The patient's father spoke at the funeral. "My daughter was recently baptized and accepted Christ as her Lord and Savior. She was always very intelligent. In two hours while being very ill and at death's door, she memorized the Lord's prayer."

The patient's father returned home to collect his belongings. He divorced his wife and moved back to his home state and lived with his sister. They both agreed that they would eventually see the patient in heaven someday. And every night the father would kneel and pray the Lord's prayer.

At the remembrance provided by the hospice, no family member showed up. However, some of the staff that cared for her did. The pastor said, "She had become a Christian on the unit and was loved and cared for by her father and staff. Before passing, she had thanked everyone for everything they did for her. Also, they all remember her father telling her, 'I love you with all my heart.'"

The End

Closing

I HOPE THIS book's stories will give you an insight into the flow of how hospice works. In my next book, I will go into detail on palliative pathways. You've just read how these pathways work. In the future, you will see how to identify these pathways and implement care for the patient, with rationale.

It is an honor to write these experiences in life. Also, I believe it is a great responsibility to provide objective information for the reader.

Sincerely,
Lawrence James

About the Author

THE AUTHOR HAS practiced nursing in several areas of health care. His specialty is hospice palliative care. Out of thirty years of nursing, 70 percent was hospice care. He also became an ordained pastor to care for his patients spiritually also. He believes that we were all put here to care for each other.